D0570905

pasta sauces

p

This is a Parragon Publishing Book
First published in 2004

Parragon Publishing
Queen Street House
4 Queen Street
Bath BA1 1HE, UK

Copyright © Parragon 2004

All rights reserved. No part of this publication may be
reproduced, stored in a retrieval system, or transmitted, in any
form or by any means, electronic, mechanical, photocopying,
recording, or otherwise, without the prior permission of the
copyright holder.

ISBN: 1-40543-649-2

Printed in China

Produced by the Bridgewater Book Company Ltd.
Project Designer: Michael Whitehead
Project Editor: Anna Samuels

Notes for the Reader
This book uses imperial, metric, or US cup measurements. Follow
the same units of measurement throughout; do not mix imperial
and metric. All spoon measurements are level: teaspoons are
assumed to be 5 ml, and tablespoons are assumed to be 15 ml.
Unless otherwise stated, milk is assumed to be whole, eggs and
individual vegetables such as potatoes are medium, and pepper
is freshly ground black pepper.

Recipes using raw or very lightly cooked eggs should be avoided
by infants, the elderly, pregnant women, convalescents, and
anyone suffering from an illness.

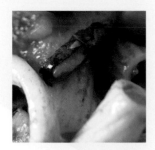

contents

introduction

PASTA is one of the easiest dishes to prepare and, combined with a meat, seafood, cheese, or vegetable sauce, it makes a delicious meal that can be eaten as a light lunch or as a substantial evening dish. The recipes are also ideal for serving on special occasions at the table or as part of a buffet meal.

Pasta is very popular and versatile. It is cheap and easy to make and can be combined with a wide variety of delicious sauces. Meat and poultry sauces, vegetable sauces, or fish and seafood sauces are all excellent pasta accompaniments.

Pasta has existed since the Roman Empire. There are over 200 different pasta types, with new shapes being invented all the time. It is crucial that you combine the right shape of pasta with its sauce. For example, the basic Italian tomato sauce is an excellent sauce for spaghetti, as it is successfully absorbed into the long thin pasta.

Tagliatelle, on the other hand, are ideal for creamy sauces such as the Garlic, Mushroom, and Cheese sauce. Pasta shapes are best suited for chunky sauces such as the Tomato, Mushroom, and Bacon sauce.

Pasta is made from durum wheat flour and is therefore a good source of protein and carbohydrate and an ideal energy source for those with busy lifestyles. Dried pasta is an ideal pantry staple that can be cooked quickly to accompany a sauce. Fresh pasta, though it cooks more quickly, cannot be stored.

To cook pasta the correct way, it is best to use a large pan that gives the pasta enough space. Allow 4 cups of water for every 4 oz/115 g pasta. Bring the water to a boil quickly and then add the salt and pasta together, stirring once. The amount of cooking time will depend on the quantity and type of pasta. The pasta will be ready when it is al dente—firm but still slightly chewy. It is easy to overcook pasta, so you need to watch out for this. Cook the sauce before you cook the pasta; if you

cook the pasta first, there is the risk that it will be cold by the time you have finished preparing the sauce! In addition to getting cold, pasta that stands for a while tends to become quite sticky.

In this book the recipes are divided up into four groups of recipes—meat and poultry sauces, seafood and fish sauces, creamy and cheesy sauces, and finally vegetable sauces.

All are recipes that you will come back to again and again, as they are fun, simple, and tasty. They are also easy to prepare and presented with clarity, from the initial preparation stages right through to the final serving of each dish. Each recipe is also accompanied by a photo that shows how versatile a dish pasta is and just how colorful pasta sauces can be.

basic tomato sauce

A sauce that is excellent for any type of pasta and a useful recipe for other dishes.

SERVES 4

2 tbsp olive oil

1 large onion, finely chopped

2 garlic cloves, crushed

10 oz/280 g canned chopped tomatoes

2 tbsp chopped fresh parsley

1 tsp dried oregano

2 bay leaves

2 tbsp tomato paste

salt and pepper

Heat the oil in a large skillet and cook the onion for 2–3 minutes, or until translucent. Add the garlic and cook for 1 minute. Stir in the chopped tomatoes, parsley, oregano, bay leaves, and tomato paste and season to taste with salt and pepper. Bring the sauce to a boil, then simmer for 15–20 minutes.

meat &
poultry sauces

MEAT and poultry sauces go particularly well with pasta and are very popular. The seven recipes in this chapter draw on a range of meats and poultry: beef, veal, chicken, lamb, bacon, and pork. The recipes are wonderfully varied, from the classic well-known Bolognese sauce to the more unusual Pumpkin Sauce with Prosciutto.

bolognese sauce

You can use this classic meat sauce both to accompany spaghetti,
and for baked pasta dishes such as lasagna and cannelloni. *SERVES 4*

1 lb/450 g dried spaghetti

1 tbsp olive oil

sauce

2 tbsp olive oil

2 garlic cloves, crushed

1 large onion, finely chopped

1 carrot, diced

**2 cups ground lean beef,
veal, or chicken**

3 oz/85 g chicken livers, finely chopped

3¹/₂ oz/100 g lean prosciutto, diced

²/₃ cup Marsala

10 oz/280 g canned chopped plum tomatoes

1 tbsp chopped fresh basil leaves

2 tbsp tomato paste

salt and pepper

To make the sauce, heat the olive oil in a large pan. Add the garlic, onion, and carrot and cook for 6 minutes.

Add the ground meat, chicken livers, and prosciutto. Cook over medium heat for 12 minutes, or until well browned.

Stir in the Marsala, tomatoes, basil, and tomato paste and cook, stirring, for 4 minutes. Season to taste. Cover the pan and simmer for 30 minutes. Remove the lid, then stir and simmer for an additional 15 minutes.

Meanwhile, to cook the pasta, bring a large pan of lightly salted water to a boil. Add the spaghetti and oil and cook for 12 minutes, or until tender but still firm to the bite. Drain and transfer to a serving dish. Pour over the sauce and serve.

variation

Chicken livers are an essential ingredient in a classic Bolognese sauce, to which they add richness. However, if you prefer not to use them, you can substitute the same quantity of ground beef, veal, or chicken.

tarragon meatball sauce

This well-loved Italian sauce is famous across the world. Make the most of it by using high-quality steak for the meatballs. *SERVES 4*

Place the brown bread crumbs in a bowl, then add the milk and set aside to soak for 30 minutes.

To make the sauce, melt half of the butter in a pan. Add the flour and cook, stirring constantly, for 2 minutes. Gradually stir in the beef stock and cook, stirring constantly, for an additional 5 minutes. Add the tomatoes, tomato paste, sugar, and tarragon, reserving a little tarragon to garnish. Season well and simmer for 25 minutes.

Meanwhile, mix the onion, ground steak, and paprika into the bread crumbs, and season to taste. Shape the mixture into 16 meatballs.

Heat the oil and remaining butter in a skillet and cook the meatballs, turning, until brown all over. Place in a deep casserole and pour over the tomato sauce, then cover and bake in a preheated oven, 350°F/180°C, for 25 minutes.

To cook the pasta, bring a large pan of lightly salted water to a boil. Add the fresh spaghetti, then bring back to a boil and cook for 2–3 minutes, or until tender but still firm to the bite.

Meanwhile, remove the meatballs from the oven and cool for 3 minutes. Serve the meatballs and their sauce with the spaghetti, garnished with the reserved tarragon.

1 lb/450 g fresh spaghetti

meatballs
3 cups brown bread crumbs
2/3 cup milk
1 large onion, chopped
1 lb/450 g ground steak
1 tsp paprika

sauce
2 tbsp butter
3 tbsp whole-wheat flour
generous 3/4 cup beef stock
14 oz/400 g canned chopped tomatoes
2 tbsp tomato paste
1 tsp sugar
1 tbsp chopped fresh tarragon
salt and pepper
4 tbsp olive oil

sun-dried tomato sauce

There is an appetizing contrast of textures and flavors in this satisfying sauce,
making it a particularly good accompaniment for pasta. *SERVES 4*

1 lb 2 oz/500 g ground lean beef

1 cup soft white bread crumbs

1 garlic clove, crushed

2 tbsp chopped fresh parsley

1 tsp dried oregano

pinch of freshly grated nutmeg

1/4 tsp ground coriander

1/2 cup freshly grated Parmesan cheese

2–3 tbsp milk

all-purpose flour, for dusting

3 tbsp olive oil

14 oz/400 g dried tagliatelle

2 tbsp butter, diced

sauce

3 tbsp olive oil

2 large onions, sliced

2 celery stalks, thinly sliced

2 garlic cloves, chopped

14 oz/400 g canned chopped tomatoes

4 1/2 oz/125 g sun-dried tomatoes in oil,
drained and chopped

2 tbsp tomato paste

1 tbsp dark muscovado sugar

about 2/3 cup white wine or water

salt and pepper

To make the sauce, heat the oil in a skillet. Add the onions and celery and cook until translucent. Add the garlic and cook for 1 minute. Stir in all the tomatoes, tomato paste, sugar, and wine and season to taste with salt and pepper. Bring to a boil and simmer for 10 minutes.

Meanwhile, break up the meat in a bowl with a wooden spoon until it becomes a sticky paste. Stir in the bread crumbs, garlic, herbs, and spices. Stir in the cheese and enough milk to make a firm paste. Flour your hands, then take large spoonfuls of the mixture and shape it into 12 balls. Heat the oil in a skillet and cook the meatballs for 5–6 minutes, or until browned.

Pour the tomato sauce over the meatballs. Lower the heat, then cover the skillet and simmer for 30 minutes, turning once or twice. Add a little extra wine if the sauce is beginning to become dry.

To cook the pasta, bring a large pan of lightly salted water to a boil. Add the pasta, then bring back to a boil and cook for 8–10 minutes, or until tender but still firm to the bite. Drain, then turn into a warmed serving dish. Dot with the butter and toss with 2 forks. Spoon the meatballs and sauce over the pasta and serve immediately.

bucatini with lamb
& yellow bell pepper sauce

This regional specialty is traditionally served with square-shape macaroni,
but this is not widely available (although you may find
it in an Italian delicatessen). This recipe uses bucatini instead. *SERVES 4*

4 tbsp olive oil

10 oz/280 g boneless lamb, cubed

1 garlic clove, finely chopped

1 bay leaf

1 cup dry white wine

salt and pepper

**2 large yellow bell peppers,
deseeded and diced**

4 tomatoes, peeled and chopped

9 oz/250 g dried bucatini

Heat half the olive oil in a large, heavy-bottom skillet. Add the cubes of lamb and cook over medium heat, stirring frequently, until browned on all sides. Add the garlic and cook for an additional 1 minute. Add the bay leaf, then pour in the wine and season to taste with salt and pepper. Bring to a boil and cook for 5 minutes, or until reduced.

Stir in the remaining oil, bell peppers, and tomatoes. Reduce the heat, then cover and simmer, stirring occasionally, for 45 minutes.

Meanwhile, bring a large, heavy-bottom pan of lightly salted water to a boil. Add the pasta, then return to a boil and cook for 8–10 minutes, or until tender but still firm to the bite. Drain and transfer to a warmed serving dish. Remove and discard the bay leaf from the lamb sauce and spoon the sauce onto the pasta. Toss well and serve immediately.

creamy chicken sauce

This creamy chicken sauce served with spinach ribbon noodles
makes a very appetizing and satisfying dish. *SERVES 4*

Make the tomato sauce, then set aside and keep
warm. To make the chicken sauce, melt the butter
in a large, heavy skillet over medium heat. Add the
chicken pieces and almonds and cook, stirring
frequently, for 5–6 minutes, or until the chicken is
cooked through.

Meanwhile, pour the cream into a small pan,
then set over low heat and bring to a boil.
Continue to boil for 10 minutes, or until reduced by
almost half. Pour the cream over the chicken and
almonds, then stir well and season with salt and
pepper to taste. Remove the pan from the heat,
then set aside and keep warm.

To cook the pasta, bring a large pan of lightly
salted water to a boil. Add the pasta, then bring
back to a boil and cook until tender but still firm
to the bite. Fresh tagliatelle will take 2–3 minutes
to cook and dried pasta will take 8–10 minutes,
timed from when the water returns to a boil. Drain
the pasta, then return to the pan. Cover and keep
warm until ready to serve.

When ready to serve, turn the pasta into a
warmed serving dish and spoon the tomato sauce
over it. Spoon the chicken and cream sauce into
the center. Sprinkle with the basil leaves and serve.

1 quantity Basic Tomato Sauce (see page 7)
8 oz/225 g fresh or dried green tagliatelle
fresh basil leaves, to garnish

sauce
4 tbsp unsalted butter
14 oz/400 g skinless, boneless chicken breast
  portions, thinly sliced
3 oz/85 g blanched almonds
1¹/4 cups heavy cream
salt and pepper

carbonara sauce

Make sure that all of the cooked ingredients are as hot as possible before adding the eggs, so that they cook on contact. *SERVES 4*

15 oz/425 g dried spaghetti
sprigs of fresh sage, to garnish
freshly grated Parmesan cheese,
to serve (optional)

sauce
1 tbsp olive oil
1 large onion, thinly sliced
2 garlic cloves, chopped
6 oz/175 g rindless bacon, cut into thin strips
2 tbsp butter
3 cups sliced mushrooms
1¼ cups heavy cream
3 eggs, beaten
1 cup freshly grated Parmesan cheese
salt and pepper

Warm a large serving dish or bowl. To cook the pasta, bring a large pan of lightly salted water to a boil. Add the spaghetti, then bring back to a boil and cook for 8–10 minutes, or until tender but still firm to the bite. Drain well, then return to the pan and keep warm.

Meanwhile, to make the sauce, heat the olive oil in a skillet over medium heat. Add the onion and cook, stirring occasionally, for 2–3 minutes, or until translucent. Add the garlic and bacon and cook until the bacon is crisp. Transfer to the warm dish or bowl.

Melt the butter in the skillet. Add the mushrooms and cook over medium heat, stirring occasionally, for 3–4 minutes, or until tender. Return the bacon mixture to the skillet. Cover and keep warm.

Combine the cream, eggs, and cheese in a large bowl and season to taste.

Working very quickly, tip the spaghetti into the bacon mixture and pour over the eggs. Toss the spaghetti quickly into the egg and cream mixture, using 2 forks, and serve immediately, garnished with sage. If you wish, serve with extra grated Parmesan cheese.

cook's tip

The key to success with this recipe is
not to overcook the egg. It is important to
keep all the ingredients hot enough to just
cook the egg and to work rapidly to avoid
scrambling it.

pumpkin sauce
with prosciutto

This unusual pasta sauce comes from the Emilia Romagna region
of Italy. Why not serve it with Lambrusco, the local wine? *SERVES 4*

To make the sauce, cut the pumpkin in half and scoop out the seeds with a spoon. Cut the pumpkin into ½-inch/1-cm dice.

Heat the olive oil in a large pan. Add the onion and garlic and cook over low heat for 3 minutes, or until soft. Add half the chopped parsley and cook for 1 minute.

Add the pumpkin pieces and cook for 2–3 minutes. Season to taste with nutmeg, and salt and pepper. Add half the stock to the pan and bring to a boil, then cover and simmer for about 10 minutes, or until the pumpkin is tender. Add more stock whenever the pumpkin is becoming dry and looks as if it might be about to burn.

Add the prosciutto to the pan and cook, stirring, for an additional 2 minutes.

Meanwhile, to cook the pasta, bring a large pan of lightly salted water to a boil. Add the tagliatelle and olive oil and cook for 12 minutes, or until tender but still firm to the bite. Drain the pasta and transfer to a warm serving dish. Stir the cream into the pumpkin and

9 oz/250 g dried green or white tagliatelle

1 tbsp olive oil

freshly grated Parmesan cheese, to serve

sauce

1 lb 2 oz/500 g pumpkin or butternut squash, peeled

2 tbsp olive oil

1 onion, finely chopped

2 garlic cloves, crushed

4–6 tbsp chopped fresh parsley

pinch of freshly grated nutmeg

salt and pepper

about 1¼ cups chicken stock or vegetable stock

4 oz/115 g prosciutto, cut into small pieces

⅔ cup heavy cream

prosciutto sauce and heat through well. Spoon the mixture over the tagliatelle, then sprinkle over the remaining parsley to garnish and serve while still hot. Serve the grated Parmesan separately.

cook's tip

Sour cream contains 18–20% fat, so if
you are following a lowfat diet you can
leave it out of this recipe or substitute
a lowfat alternative.

tomato, mushroom & bacon sauce

In this dish, fresh tomatoes make a delicious Italian-style sauce, which goes particularly well with pasta. *SERVES 2*

1 tbsp olive oil

1 small onion, finely chopped

1–2 garlic cloves, crushed

12 oz/350 g tomatoes, peeled and chopped

2 tsp tomato paste

2 tbsp water

salt and pepper

10¹/₂ –12 oz/300–350 g dried pasta shapes

3¹/₄ oz/90 g lean bacon, de-rinded and diced

³/₄ cup sliced mushrooms

1 tbsp chopped fresh parsley or 1 tsp chopped cilantro

2 tbsp sour cream or natural mascarpone (optional)

Heat the olive oil in a pan and cook the onion and garlic gently over low heat until soft.

Add the tomatoes, tomato paste, and water to the mixture in the pan, then season with salt and pepper to taste and bring to a boil. Cover and simmer gently for 10 minutes.

Meanwhile, cook the pasta in a large pan of boiling salted water for 8–10 minutes, or until just tender. Drain thoroughly and then transfer to warm serving dishes.

Heat the bacon gently in a skillet until the fat runs. Add the mushrooms and continue cooking for 3–4 minutes. Drain off any excess fat.

Add the bacon and mushrooms to the tomato mixture, together with the parsley and the sour cream, if using. Reheat and serve with the pasta.

seafood &
fish sauces

SEAFOOD and fish make excellent ingredients in pasta sauces. The six recipes here draw on a wide range of seafood (shrimp, squid, mussels, crab, and clams) and offer an array of different flavors. The seven fish sauces include two tasty smoked salmon recipes, a sardine-based sauce, and three delicious anchovy-based sauces.

seafood sauce

Fresh clams are available from most good fish dealers. If you prefer, use canned clams, which are less messy to eat but not so pretty to serve. *SERVES 4*

1 lb 8 oz/675 g fresh pasta,
or 12 oz/350 g dried pasta

sauce

1 lb 8 oz/675 g fresh clams,
or 10 oz/280 g canned clams, drained
2 tbsp olive oil

2 garlic cloves, finely chopped

14 oz/400 g mixed prepared seafood, such as shrimp, squid, and mussels, defrosted if frozen

$^2/_3$ cup white wine

$^2/_3$ cup fish stock

2 tbsp chopped fresh tarragon

salt and pepper

First make the sauce. If you are using fresh clams, you need to scrub them clean and discard any that are already open.

Heat the oil in a large skillet. Add the garlic and clams and cook for 2 minutes, shaking the skillet to ensure that all of the clams are coated in the oil. Add the remaining seafood to the skillet and cook for an additional 2 minutes.

Pour the wine and stock over the mixed seafood and garlic and bring to a boil. Cover the skillet, then lower the heat and simmer for 8–10 minutes, or until the shells open. Discard any clams or mussels that do not open.

To cook the pasta, place in a pan of boiling water and cook according to the directions on the package, or until tender but still firm to the bite. Drain.

Stir the tarragon into the sauce and season to taste. Transfer the pasta to a serving plate and pour over the sauce.

variation

Red Seafood Sauce can be made by adding
$1/2$ cup tomato paste to the sauce along with
the stock. Follow the same cooking method.

shrimp & vegetable sauce

Shelled shrimp from the freezer can become the star ingredient in
this colorful and tasty sauce. *SERVES 4*

To cook the pasta, bring a pan of lightly salted water to a boil. Add the spaghetti and half of the olive oil and cook until tender but still firm to the bite. Drain the spaghetti, then return to the pan and toss with the remaining olive oil. Cover and keep warm.

To make the sauce, bring the chicken stock and lemon juice to a boil. Add the cauliflower and carrots and cook for 3–4 minutes. Lift out of the pan and set aside. Add the snow peas to the pan and cook for 1–2 minutes. Remove and set aside with the other vegetables.

Melt half the butter in a skillet over medium heat. Add the onion and zucchini and cook for about 3 minutes. Add the garlic and shelled shrimp and cook for an additional 2–3 minutes, or until thoroughly heated through.

Add the reserved vegetables and heat through, stirring. Season to taste and stir in the remaining butter.

Transfer the spaghetti to a warm serving dish. Pour over the sauce and add the chopped parsley. Toss well with 2 forks until coated. Sprinkle over the Parmesan cheese and paprika, then garnish with the whole shrimp and serve immediately.

8 oz/225 g dried spaghetti, broken into
6-inch/15-cm pieces

2 tbsp olive oil

2 tbsp chopped fresh parsley

1/4 cup freshly grated Parmesan cheese

1/2 tsp paprika

4 whole cooked shrimp, to garnish

sauce

1 1/4 cups chicken stock

1 tsp lemon juice

1 small cauliflower, cut into florets

2 carrots, thinly sliced

generous 1 cup snow peas

4 tbsp butter

1 onion, sliced

8 oz/225 g zucchini, sliced

1 garlic clove, chopped

12 oz/350 g cooked, shelled shrimp

salt and pepper

spicy crab sauce

This sauce is probably one of the simplest in the book, yet the result is as impressive as a sauce that takes a long time to prepare. *SERVES 4*

12 oz/350 g dried spaghettini

salt and pepper

lemon wedges, to garnish

sauce

1 dressed crab, about 1 lb/450 g (including the shell)

6 tbsp extra-virgin olive oil

1 fresh red chili, deseeded and finely chopped

2 garlic cloves, finely chopped

3 tbsp chopped fresh parsley

2 tbsp lemon juice

1 tsp finely grated lemon zest

Scoop the meat from the crab shell into a bowl. Mix the white and brown meat lightly together and set aside.

To cook the pasta, bring a large pan of lightly salted water to a boil. Add the pasta, then bring back to a boil and cook for 8–10 minutes, or until tender but still firm to the bite. Drain well and return to the pan.

To make the sauce, heat 2 tablespoons of the olive oil in a skillet. Add the chili and garlic. Cook for 30 seconds, then add the crab meat, parsley, lemon juice, and lemon zest. Cook over low heat for an additional 1 minute, or until the crab meat is just heated through.

Add the crab sauce to the pasta with the remaining olive oil and season to taste with salt and pepper. Toss together thoroughly, then transfer to a warmed serving dish. Serve immediately, garnished with lemon wedges.

cook's tip

If you prefer to buy your own fresh crab,
you will need a large crab weighing
about 2 lb 4 oz/1 kg.

saffron mussel sauce

Saffron is the most expensive spice in the world, but you only ever need
a small quantity. This sauce is delicious with tagliatelle or other ribbon pasta. *SERVES 4*

To make the sauce, scrub and debeard the mussels under cold running water. Discard any that do not close when sharply tapped. Put the mussels in a pan with the wine and onion. Cover and cook over high heat, shaking the pan, for 5–8 minutes, or until the shells open.

Drain and reserve the cooking liquid. Discard any mussels that are still closed. Reserve a few mussels in their shells for the garnish and remove the remainder from their shells.

Strain the cooking liquid into a pan. Bring to a boil and reduce by about half, then remove from the heat.

Melt the butter in a pan. Add the garlic and cook, stirring frequently, for 2 minutes or until golden brown. Stir in the cornstarch and cook, stirring, for 1 minute. Gradually stir in the cooking liquid and the cream. Crush the saffron threads and add to the pan. Season with salt and pepper to taste and simmer over low heat for 2–3 minutes, or until thickened.

Stir in the egg yolk, lemon juice, and shelled mussels. Do not let the mixture boil.

To cook the pasta, bring a pan of lightly salted water to a boil. Add the pasta and oil and cook according to the directions on the package, until tender but still firm to the bite. Drain and transfer to a serving dish. Add the mussel sauce and toss together. Garnish with the chopped parsley and reserved mussels and serve.

1 lb/450 g dried tagliatelle

1 tbsp olive oil

3 tbsp chopped fresh parsley, to garnish

sauce

2 lb 4 oz/1 kg mussels

²/₃ cup white wine

1 medium onion, finely chopped

2 tbsp butter

2 garlic cloves, crushed

2 tsp cornstarch

1¹/₄ cups heavy cream

pinch of saffron threads or saffron powder

salt and pepper

1 egg yolk

juice of ¹/₂ lemon

clam sauce

This is another cook-in-a-hurry recipe that transforms pantry ingredients into a dish with style. *SERVES 4*

14 oz/400 g vermicelli, spaghetti, or other long pasta

2 tbsp butter

1 tbsp olive oil

2 onions, chopped

2 garlic cloves, chopped

14 oz/400 g clams in brine

¹/₂ cup white wine

4 tbsp chopped parsley

¹/₂ tsp dried oregano

pinch of grated nutmeg

salt and pepper

sprigs of fresh basil, to garnish

2 tbsp shaved Parmesan, to serve

Bring a large pan of lightly salted water to a boil. Add the pasta, then bring back to a boil and cook for 8–10 minutes, or until tender but firm to the bite. Drain well. Return to the pan and add the butter. Cover and shake. Set the pan aside and keep warm.

Heat the olive oil in a pan. Add the onions and cook over low heat, stirring occasionally, for 5 minutes, or until softened. Stir in the garlic and cook for another minute.

Strain the liquid from the clams and pour half of it into the pan. Discard the remaining liquid and reserve the clams.

Add the wine to the pan. Bring to simmering point, stirring constantly, and simmer for 3 minutes.

Add the clams and herbs to the pan and season to taste with nutmeg and pepper. Lower the heat and cook until the sauce is heated through.

Transfer the pasta to a warmed serving platter and pour the clam sauce over it.

Garnish with sprigs of basil and sprinkle over the Parmesan. Serve hot.

rigatoni with
squid sauce

This delicious combination of pasta and squid is excellent for a light summer supper.
If time is limited, use fresh pasta, as it takes less time to cook than dried.
Farfalle and penne would also work well. *SERVES 4*

1 red bell pepper

1 yellow bell pepper

1 tbsp corn oil

12 oz/350 g prepared squid rings

1 onion, chopped

1 garlic clove, finely chopped

14 oz/400 g canned chopped tomatoes

1/2–1 tsp chili powder

9 oz/250 g dried rigatoni

2 tbsp chopped fresh basil

salt and pepper

Preheat the broiler to medium. Place the bell peppers on a baking sheet and roast under the broiler, turning frequently, for 15 minutes, or until charred and beginning to blacken. Remove with tongs, then place in a plastic bag and seal the top. When the bell peppers are cool enough to handle, rub off the skins and deseed, then chop the flesh.

Heat the oil in a heavy-bottom skillet. Add the squid rings and stir-fry for 1–2 minutes, or until opaque. Remove the squid and set aside. Add the onion and garlic and cook for 5 minutes, or until soft. Add the tomatoes and bell peppers and chili powder to taste, then reduce the heat and simmer for 20–25 minutes, or until thickened.

Meanwhile, cook the pasta in a pan of lightly salted water for 8–10 minutes, or until tender but still firm to the bite. Just before serving, stir the squid rings and basil into the sauce and season to taste with salt and pepper. Heat through for 2–3 minutes. Drain the pasta, then transfer to a serving dish and toss with the sauce. Serve.

variation

Use fresh tomatoes instead of canned
when they are in season. Peel, deseed,
and chop 1 lb 10 oz/750 g tomatoes.

cook's tip

Serve this rich and luxurious
dish with salad greens tossed
in a lemon-flavored dressing.

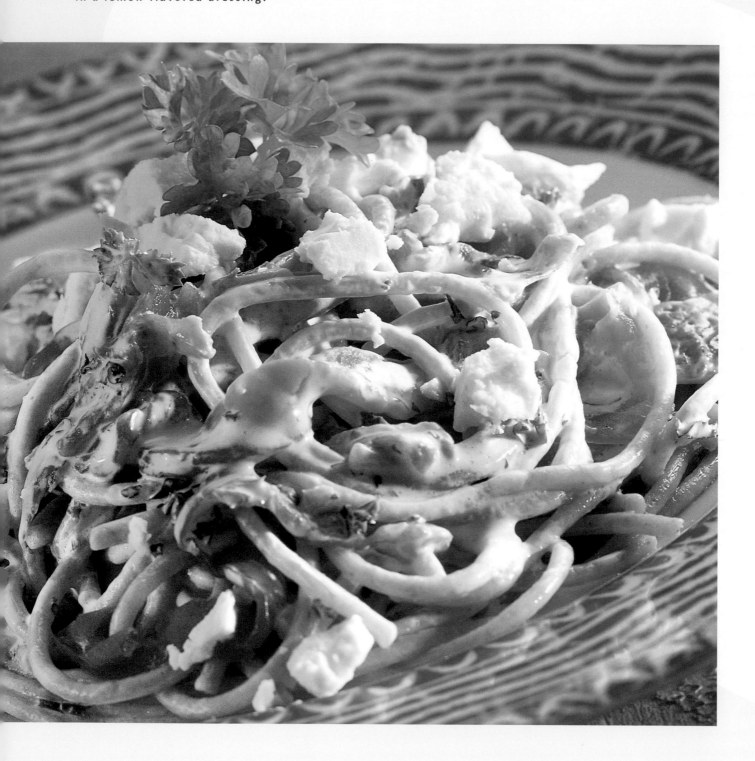

smoked salmon cream sauce

This luxurious sauce is made in moments, and can be used to astonish and delight any unexpected guests. *SERVES 4*

1 lb/450 g dried white or
buckwheat spaghetti

2 tbsp olive oil

to garnish

3¹/₄ oz/90 g feta cheese,
well drained and crumbled

sprigs of fresh cilantro or parsley

sauce

1¹/₄ cups heavy cream

²/₃ cup whisky or brandy

4¹/₂ oz/125 g smoked salmon

pinch of cayenne pepper

black pepper

2 tbsp chopped fresh cilantro or parsley

To cook the pasta, bring a large pan of lightly salted water to a boil. Add the spaghetti and half of the olive oil and cook until tender but still firm to the bite. Drain the spaghetti, then return to the pan and sprinkle over the remaining olive oil. Cover and shake the pan, then set aside and keep warm.

To make the sauce, pour the cream into a small pan and bring to simmering point, but do not let it boil. Pour the whisky into another small pan and bring to simmering point, but do not let it boil. Remove both pans from the heat and mix the cream with the whisky.

Cut the smoked salmon into thin strips and add to the cream sauce. Season to taste with cayenne and black pepper. Just before serving,

stir in the chopped cilantro. Transfer the spaghetti to a warm serving dish, then pour over the sauce and toss thoroughly with 2 large forks. To garnish, scatter over the crumbled feta cheese and sprigs of cilantro, then serve immediately.

variation

Substitute the same amount of arugula for
the watercress, if you like, and garnish with
a few sprigs of fresh flatleaf parsley.

smoked salmon & watercress sauce

This simple dish takes just moments to make, looks lovely, tastes fabulous, and contains absolutely no saturated fat—what more could you possibly want? *SERVES 4*

Bring a large pan of lightly salted water to a boil over medium heat. Add the pasta, then return to a boil and cook for 8–10 minutes, or until tender but still firm to the bite.

Meanwhile, heat the olive oil in a large nonstick skillet. Add the garlic and cook over low heat, stirring constantly, for 30 seconds. Add the salmon and watercress, then season to taste with pepper and cook for an additional 30 seconds, or until the watercress has wilted.

Drain the cooked pasta and return to the pan. Mix the salmon and watercress with the pasta. Toss the mixture using 2 large forks. Divide between 4 large serving plates and garnish with extra watercress leaves. Serve immediately.

salt and pepper

8 oz/225 g dried fettuccine

1 tsp olive oil

1 garlic clove, finely chopped

**2 oz/55 g smoked salmon,
cut into thin strips**

**2 oz/55 g watercress leaves,
plus extra to garnish**

sardine & fennel sauce

This is a very quick sauce and is ideal paired with pasta for midweek suppers because it is so simple to prepare, yet packed full of flavor. *SERVES 4*

12 oz/350 g dried linguine

2 tbsp olive oil

sprigs of fresh parsley, to garnish

sauce

8 sardines, filleted

1 fennel bulb

2 tbsp olive oil

3 garlic cloves, sliced

1 tsp chili flakes

1/2 tsp finely grated lemon zest

1 tbsp lemon juice

2 tbsp pine nuts, toasted

2 tbsp chopped fresh parsley

salt and pepper

To make the sauce, wash the sardines and pat dry on paper towels. Coarsely chop them into large pieces and set aside. Trim the fennel bulb and slice very thinly.

Heat the olive oil in a large, heavy-bottom skillet and add the sliced garlic and the chili flakes. Cook for 1 minute, then add the fennel slices. Cook over a medium-high heat, stirring occasionally, for 4–5 minutes, or until softened. Lower the heat, then add the sardine pieces and cook for an additional 3–4 minutes, or until just cooked.

To cook the pasta, bring a pan of lightly salted water to a boil. Add the pasta, then bring back to a boil and cook for 8–10 minutes, or until tender but still firm to the bite. Drain well and return to the pan.

Add the lemon zest and juice, pine nuts, and parsley to the sauce and toss together. Season. Add the sauce to the pasta with the remaining olive oil and toss together gently. Transfer to a warmed serving dish, then garnish with parsley and serve.

cook's tip

Reserve a couple of tablespoons of the pasta
cooking water and add to the pasta with the
sauce if the mixture seems a little dry.

variation
Substitute generous ¹/₃ cup chopped fresh
basil for half the parsley, and garnish
with capers instead of black olives.

tuna & anchovy sauce

The delicious parsley sauce in this recipe enhances the classic
Italian combination of pasta and tuna. *SERVES 4*

To make the sauce, first remove any bones from the tuna. Put the tuna into a food processor or blender. Add the anchovies, oil, and parsley. Process until very smooth.

Spoon the sour cream into the food processor or blender and process again for a few seconds to blend thoroughly. Season with salt and pepper to taste.

To cook the pasta, bring a large pan of lightly salted water to a boil. Add the spaghetti and olive oil and cook for 8–10 minutes, or until tender but still firm to the bite.

Drain the spaghetti, then return to the pan and place over medium heat. Add the butter and toss well to coat. Spoon in the sauce and quickly toss into the spaghetti, mixing well using 2 forks.

Remove the pan from the heat and divide the spaghetti between warm individual serving plates. Garnish with olives and parsley and serve with warm, crusty bread.

1 lb/450 g dried spaghetti

1 tbsp olive oil

2 tbsp butter

pitted black olives, to garnish

warm crusty bread, to serve

sauce

7 oz/200 g canned tuna, drained

2¹/4 oz/60 g canned anchovies, drained

1 cup olive oil

1 cup flatleaf parsley, coarsely chopped,
    plus extra to garnish

²/3 cup sour cream

salt and pepper

spinach & anchovy sauce

This colorful light sauce can be paired with different types of pasta,
including fettucine, spaghetti, and linguine. *SERVES 4*

14 oz/400 g dried fettucine

salt

1 tbsp olive oil

sauce

2 lb/900 g fresh, young spinach leaves

4 tbsp olive oil

3 tbsp pine nuts

3 garlic cloves, crushed

8 canned anchovy fillets, drained
    and chopped

To make the sauce, trim off any tough spinach stems. Rinse the spinach leaves and then place them in a large pan with only the water that is clinging to them after washing. Cover and cook over high heat, shaking the pan from time to time, until the spinach has wilted but retains its color. Drain well, then set aside and keep warm.

To cook the pasta, bring a large pan of lightly salted water to a boil. Add the fettucine, then bring back to a boil and cook for 8–10 minutes, or until tender but still firm to the bite.

Meanwhile, going back to the sauce, heat the olive oil in a pan. Add the pine nuts and cook until golden. Remove the pine nuts from the pan with a slotted spoon and set aside.

Add the garlic to the pan and cook until golden. Add the anchovies and stir in the spinach. Cook, stirring constantly, for 2–3 minutes, or until heated through. Return the pine nuts to the pan.

Drain the fettucine, then toss in olive oil and transfer to a warm serving dish. Spoon the anchovy and spinach sauce over the fettucine, then toss lightly and serve immediately.

cook's tip

If you are in a hurry, you can use frozen
spinach. Thaw and drain it thoroughly,
pressing out as much moisture as possible.
Cut the leaves into strips and add to the
dish with the anchovies.

pesto & anchovy sauce

This is an ideal dish for cooks in a hurry because it can be prepared in minutes from pantry ingredients. *SERVES 4*

6 tbsp olive oil

2 garlic cloves, crushed

2¹/₄ oz/60 g canned anchovy fillets, drained

1 lb/450 g dried spaghetti

2¹/₄ oz/60 g ready-made pesto sauce

2 tbsp finely chopped fresh oregano

salt and pepper

generous ³/₄ cup grated Parmesan cheese, plus extra to garnish (optional)

sprigs of fresh oregano, to garnish

Heat 5 tablespoons of the oil in a small pan. Add the garlic and cook for 3 minutes.

Lower the heat, then stir in the anchovies and cook, stirring occasionally, for 10–12 minutes, or until the anchovies have disintegrated.

Bring a large pan of lightly salted water to a boil. Add the spaghetti and the remaining olive oil and cook for 8–10 minutes, or until just tender but still firm to the bite.

Add the pesto sauce and chopped oregano to the garlic and anchovy mixture, and season with pepper to taste.

Drain the spaghetti and use a slotted spoon to transfer to a warm serving dish. Pour the pesto sauce over the spaghetti and then sprinkle over the grated Parmesan cheese.

Garnish with sprigs of fresh oregano, and extra Parmesan cheese, if using.

cook's tip

If you find canned anchovies too salty, soak
them in a saucer of cold milk for 5 minutes,
then drain and pat dry with paper towels
before using. The milk absorbs the salt.

cook's tip

If you are making fresh pasta, remember
that pasta dough prefers warm conditions
and responds well to handling. Do not
let chill and do not use a marble
counter for kneading.

sicilian sauce

This Sicilian sauce of anchovies mixed with pine nuts, golden raisins, and tomatoes is delicious with all types of pasta. *SERVES 4*

To make the sauce, cook the tomatoes under a preheated broiler for 10 minutes. Let cool. When cool enough to handle, peel off the skin and dice the flesh.

Place the pine nuts on a baking sheet and lightly toast under the broiler for 2–3 minutes, or until golden.

Soak the golden raisins in a bowl of warm water for about 20 minutes. Drain thoroughly.

Place the tomatoes, toasted pine nuts, and golden raisins in a small pan and heat gently.

Add the anchovies and tomato paste, heating the sauce for an additional 2–3 minutes, or until hot.

To cook the pasta, place in a pan of lightly salted boiling water and cook according to the directions on the package, or until tender but still firm to the bite. Drain thoroughly.

Transfer the pasta to a serving plate and serve with the hot sauce.

1 lb 8 oz/675 g fresh penne
or 12 oz/350 g dried penne

sauce
1 lb/450 g tomatoes, halved
2 tbsp pine nuts
scant ¹/₃ cup golden raisins
1³/₄ oz/50 g canned anchovies, drained and halved lengthwise
2 tbsp concentrated tomato paste

creamy &
cheesy sauces

TAGLIATELLE, fettuccine, tagliarini, and penne are excellent pastas for creamy and cheesy sauces. The delicious recipes included here are simple and quick to prepare and offer a diversity of flavors in their use of Parmesan, ricotta, Gorgonzola, and mascarpone cheeses.

PART THREE

creamy cheese sauce

This simple, traditional dish can be made with any long pasta, but is especially good with flat noodles, such as fettuccine or tagliatelle. *SERVES 4*

¹/₄ stick butter

generous ³/₄ cup heavy cream

1 lb/450 g fresh fettuccine

1 tbsp olive oil

³/₄ cup freshly grated Parmesan cheese,
plus extra to serve

pinch of freshly grated nutmeg

salt and pepper

fresh parsley sprigs, to garnish

Put the butter and ²/₃ cup of the cream in a large pan and bring the mixture to a boil over medium heat. Reduce the heat and then simmer gently for about 1¹/₂ minutes, or until slightly thickened.

Meanwhile, bring a large pan of lightly salted water to a boil. Add the fettuccine and olive oil and cook for 2–3 minutes, or until tender but still firm to the bite. Drain the fettuccine, then pour over the cream sauce.

Toss the fettuccine in the sauce over low heat until thoroughly coated.

Add the remaining cream, the Parmesan cheese, and nutmeg to the fettuccine mixture and season to taste with salt and pepper. Toss thoroughly to coat while gently heating through.

Transfer the fettucine mixture to a warm serving plate and garnish with the fresh sprigs of parsley. Serve immediately, handing round extra grated Parmesan cheese separately.

variation

This classic Roman dish is delicious
served with the addition of fresh peas.
Add 2 cups of shelled cooked peas with
the Parmesan cheese.

variation

**You don't have to use tagliatelle for this recipe.
You can make any type of pasta you wish.**

tagliatelle
with garlic butter

Pasta is not difficult to make yourself, just a little time-consuming.
However, the resulting pasta takes only a couple of minutes to cook and
tastes wonderful. *SERVES 4*

3 cups white bread flour,
plus extra for dusting
2 tsp salt
4 eggs, beaten
2 tbsp olive oil
scant 3/4 stick butter, melted
3 garlic cloves, finely chopped
2 tbsp chopped fresh parsley
pepper

Sift the flour into a large bowl and stir in the salt. Make a well in the center of the dry ingredients and add the eggs and the olive oil. Using a wooden spoon, stir in the eggs, gradually drawing in the flour. After a few minutes, the dough will be too stiff to use a spoon so use your fingers.

When the flour has been incorporated, turn the dough out onto a floured counter and knead for 5 minutes. If the dough is too wet, add a little flour and continue kneading. Cover with plastic wrap and let rest for at least 15 minutes.

Roll out the pasta thinly and create the pasta shapes required. This can be done by hand or using a pasta machine. To make the tagliatelle by hand, fold the thinly rolled pasta sheets into 3 and cut out long, thin strips, 1/2 inch/1 cm wide.

To cook, bring a large, heavy-bottom pan of water to a boil. Add the pasta, then return to a boil and cook for 2–3 minutes, or until tender but still firm to the bite. Drain.

Mix the butter, garlic, and parsley together. Stir into the pasta, then season with a little pepper to taste and serve immediately.

garlic, mushroom & cheese sauce

This dish can be prepared in minutes—the intense flavors are sure to make this a popular recipe. *SERVES 4*

2 tbsp walnut oil

1 bunch scallions, sliced

2 garlic cloves, thinly sliced

8 oz/225 g mushrooms, sliced

1 lb/450 g fresh green and white tagliatelle

8 oz/225 g frozen chopped leaf spinach, thawed and drained

1/2 cup full-fat cream cheese with garlic and herbs

4 tbsp light cream

salt and pepper

1/2 cup unsalted pistachios, chopped

2 tbsp shredded fresh basil

sprigs of fresh basil, to garnish

fresh Italian bread, to serve

Gently heat the walnut oil in a wok or skillet and sauté the scallions and garlic for 1 minute, or until just soft. Add the mushrooms to the skillet and stir well, then cover and cook gently for 5 minutes, or until soft.

Meanwhile, bring a large pan of lightly salted water to a boil and cook the pasta for 3–5 minutes, or until just tender. Drain the pasta thoroughly and return to the pan.

Add the spinach to the mushrooms and heat through for 1–2 minutes. Add the cheese and let it melt slightly. Stir in the cream and continue to heat without letting it boil.

Pour the vegetable mixture over the pasta, then season to taste and mix well. Heat gently, stirring, for 2–3 minutes.

Transfer the pasta into a warmed serving bowl and sprinkle over the pistachios and shredded basil. Garnish with sprigs of fresh basil and serve with fresh Italian bread.

creamy mushroom sauce

This easy vegetarian sauce is ideal for busy people with little time
to spare and it tastes very good! *SERVES 4*

To make the sauce, heat the butter and olive oil in a large pan. Add the sliced shallots and cook over medium heat for 3 minutes. Add the mushrooms and cook over low heat for 2 minutes. Season to taste with salt and pepper, then sprinkle over the flour and cook, stirring constantly, for 1 minute.

Gradually stir in the cream and port, then add the sun-dried tomatoes and a pinch of grated nutmeg. Cook over low heat for 8 minutes.

Meanwhile, to cook the pasta, bring a large pan of lightly salted water to a boil. Add the spaghetti and olive oil and cook for 12–14 minutes, or until tender but still firm to the bite.

Drain the spaghetti and return to the pan. Pour over the mushroom sauce and cook for 3 minutes. Transfer the spaghetti and mushroom sauce to a large serving plate and sprinkle over the chopped parsley. Serve with crispy triangles of fried bread.

1 lb/450 g dried spaghetti

1 tbsp olive oil

1 tbsp coarsely chopped fresh parsley

6 triangles of fried white bread, to serve

sauce

4 tbsp butter

1 tbsp olive oil

6 shallots, sliced

1 lb/450 g white mushrooms, sliced

salt and pepper

1 tsp all-purpose flour

2/3 cup heavy cream

2 tbsp port

2 cups sun-dried tomatoes, chopped

pinch of freshly grated nutmeg

variation

If you like the sound of this recipe but do
not have any port available, you can use
2 tablespoons of dry white wine instead.

cook's tip

Use 2 large forks to toss spaghetti or other
long pasta, so that it is thoroughly coated
with the sauce. Special spaghetti forks are
available from some cookware departments
and kitchen stores.

ricotta sauce

This light pasta dish has a delicate flavor ideally suited to a summer lunch. *SERVES 4*

12 oz/350 g dried spaghetti

3 tbsp butter

2 tbsp chopped fresh flatleaf parsley

generous 3/4 cup freshly ground almonds

1/2 cup ricotta cheese

pinch of freshly grated nutmeg

pinch of ground cinnamon

2/3 cup sour cream

2 tbsp olive oil

1/2 cup hot chicken stock

salt and pepper

1 tbsp pine nuts

sprigs of fresh flatleaf parsley, to garnish

Bring a pan of lightly salted water to a boil. Add the spaghetti, then bring back to a boil and cook for 8–10 minutes, or until tender but still firm to the bite.

Drain the pasta, then return to the pan and toss with the butter and chopped parsley. Set aside and keep warm.

Combine the ground almonds, ricotta cheese, nutmeg, cinnamon, and sour cream in a small pan and stir over low heat to a thick paste. Gradually stir in the oil. When the oil has been fully incorporated, gradually stir in the hot stock until smooth. Season to taste with pepper.

Transfer the spaghetti to a warm serving dish, then pour the sauce over it and toss together well (see cook's tip). Sprinkle over the pine nuts and garnish with the sprigs of fresh flatleaf parsley. Serve immediately.

tagliarini
with gorgonzola sauce

This simple, creamy pasta sauce is a classic Italian recipe. You could use Danish blue cheese instead of the Gorgonzola, if you prefer. *SERVES 4*

¹/₄ stick butter	1 tsp cornstarch
8 oz/225 g Gorgonzola cheese, coarsely crumbled	4 fresh sage sprigs, finely chopped
	salt and white pepper
²/₃ cup heavy cream	14 oz/400 g dried tagliarini
2 tbsp dry white wine	2 tbsp olive oil

Melt the butter in a heavy-bottom pan. Stir in 6 oz/175 g of the cheese and melt, over low heat, for about 2 minutes.

Add the cream, white wine, and cornstarch and beat with a whisk until fully incorporated.

Stir in the sage and season to taste with salt and white pepper. Bring to a boil over low heat, whisking constantly, until the sauce thickens. Remove from the heat and set aside while you cook the pasta.

Bring a large pan of lightly salted water to a boil. Add the tagliarini and 1 tablespoon of the olive oil. Cook the pasta for 8–10 minutes, or until just tender, then drain thoroughly and toss in the remaining olive oil. Transfer the pasta to a serving dish and keep warm.

Reheat the Gorgonzola sauce over low heat, whisking constantly. Spoon the sauce over the tagliarini, then generously sprinkle over the remaining cheese and serve.

cook's tip

When buying Gorgonzola, always check
that it is creamy yellow with delicate green
veining. Avoid hard or discolored cheese.
It should have a rich, piquant aroma,
not a bitter smell.

blue cheese & vegetable sauce

Some of the simplest and most satisfying dishes are made with pasta, such as this
delicious combination of tagliatelle with two-cheese sauce. *SERVES 4*

**10¹/₂ oz/300 g dried tagliatelle tricolore
(plain, spinach- and tomato-flavored noodles)
8 oz/225 g broccoli, broken into small florets
1¹/₂ cups mascarpone cheese
4¹/₂ oz/125 g blue cheese, chopped
1 tbsp chopped fresh oregano
salt and pepper
¹/₄ stick butter
sprigs of fresh oregano, to garnish
freshly grated Parmesan, to serve**

Cook the tagliatelle in plenty of boiling salted
water for 8–10 minutes, or until just tender.

Meanwhile, cook the broccoli florets in a
small amount of lightly salted, boiling water. Avoid
overcooking the broccoli, so that it retains much of
its color and texture.

Heat the mascarpone and blue cheeses
together gently in a large pan until they are
melted. Stir in the oregano and season with salt
and pepper to taste.

Drain the pasta thoroughly. Return it to the
pan and add the butter, tossing the tagliatelle to
coat it. Drain the broccoli well and add to the pasta
with the sauce, tossing gently to mix.

Divide the pasta between 4 warmed serving
plates. Garnish with sprigs of fresh oregano and
serve with freshly grated Parmesan.

creamy butternut squash sauce

The creamy, nutty flavor of squash complements the al dente texture of the pasta perfectly. *SERVES 4*

To make the garlic crumbs, mix the oil, garlic, and bread crumbs and spread out on a plate. Cook in the microwave on High power for 4–5 minutes, stirring until crisp and starting to brown. Reserve.

Dice the squash, then place in a large bowl with half the water. Cover and cook on High power for 8–9 minutes, stirring occasionally. Let stand for 2 minutes.

Place the pasta in a large bowl, then add a little salt and pour over enough boiling water to cover by 1 inch/2.5 cm. Cover and cook on High power for 5 minutes, stirring once, until the pasta is just tender but still firm to the bite. Let stand, covered, for 1 minute before draining.

Place the butter and onion in a large bowl. Cover and cook on High power for 3 minutes.

Using a fork, coarsely mash the squash. Add to the onion with the pasta, ham, cream, cheese, parsley, and remaining water. Season generously and mix well. Cover and cook on High power for 4 minutes, or until heated through.

Transfer the pasta to a large, warmed serving dish. Sprinkle with the garlic crumbs and serve.

2 tbsp olive oil

1 garlic clove, crushed

1 cup fresh white bread crumbs

1 lb 2 oz/500 g butternut squash, peeled and deseeded

8 tbsp water

1 lb 2 oz/500 g fresh penne, or other pasta shapes

1/8 stick butter

1 onion, sliced

4 1/2 oz/125 g ham, cut into strips

generous 3/4 cup light cream

1/2 cup freshly grated Cheddar cheese

2 tbsp chopped fresh parsley

salt and pepper

buttered pea
& cheese sauce

This delicious sauce is served with paglia e fieno ("straw and hay" pasta), which refers to the colors of the pasta when mixed together. *SERVES 4*

1 lb/450 g mixed fresh green and white
spaghetti or tagliatelle
shavings of Parmesan cheese, to garnish

sauce
4 tbsp butter
1 lb/450 g fresh peas, shelled
generous 3/4 cup heavy cream
1/2 cup freshly grated Parmesan cheese
pinch of freshly grated nutmeg
salt and pepper

To make the sauce, melt the butter in a large pan. Add the peas and cook over low heat for 2–3 minutes.

Pour 2/3 cup of the cream into the pan, then bring to a boil and simmer for 1–1¹/² minutes, or until slightly thickened. Remove the pan from the heat.

Meanwhile, to cook the pasta, bring a large pan of lightly salted water to a boil. Add the pasta, then bring back to a boil and cook for 2–3 minutes, or until just tender but still firm to the bite.

Remove the pan from the heat, then drain the pasta thoroughly and return to the pan.

Add the sauce to the pasta. Return the pan to the heat and add the remaining cream and the Parmesan cheese. Season to taste with nutmeg and salt and pepper.

While heating through, use 2 forks to toss the pasta gently so that it is coated with the sauce.

Transfer the pasta to a warmed serving dish and serve immediately, garnished with the shavings of Parmesan cheese.

variation
Cook 2¹/₂ cups sliced white or oyster
mushrooms in about 4 tablespoons of butter
over low heat for 4–5 minutes. Stir into
the sauce just before adding to the pasta.

vegetable sauces

THE ten colorful vegetable sauces included here are very easy and quick to prepare. The sauces, which can be wonderfully rich, very light, sweet, and even hot and spicy, will appeal to vegetarians and meat-eaters alike.

olive oil
& herb sauce

This easy and satisfying Roman dish originated as a cheap meal for
the impoverished, but is now a favorite in restaurants and trattorias. *SERVES 4*

¹/₂ cup olive oil

3 garlic cloves, crushed

salt and pepper

1 lb/450 g fresh spaghetti

3 tbsp coarsely chopped fresh parsley

Reserve 1 tablespoon of the olive oil and heat the remainder in a medium pan. Add the garlic and a pinch of salt and cook over low heat, stirring constantly, until golden brown, then remove the pan from the heat. Do not let the garlic burn, as this will taint its flavor. (If it does burn, you will have to start all over again!)

Meanwhile, bring a large pan of lightly salted water to a boil. Add the spaghetti and remaining olive oil and cook for 2–3 minutes, or until tender but still firm to the bite. Drain the spaghetti thoroughly and return to the pan.

Add the oil and garlic mixture to the spaghetti and toss to coat thoroughly. Season to taste with pepper, then add the chopped fresh parsley and toss well to coat again.

Transfer the spaghetti to a warm serving dish and serve immediately.

cook's tip

It is worth buying the best-quality olive oil
for dishes such as this one, which make a
feature of its flavor. Extra-virgin oil is
produced from the first pressing, and has
the lowest acidity and the finest flavor.

garlic walnut sauce

This rich pasta sauce is for garlic lovers everywhere. It is quick
and easy to prepare and full of flavor. *SERVES 4*

1 lb/450 g fresh green and white tagliatelle

salt and pepper

sprigs of fresh basil, to garnish

Italian bread, such as focaccia or
ciabatta, to serve

sauce

2 tbsp walnut oil

1 bunch of scallions, sliced

2 garlic cloves, thinly sliced

8 oz/225 g mushrooms, sliced

8 oz/225 g frozen spinach, thawed
and drained

1/2 cup full-fat cream cheese with garlic
and herbs

4 tbsp light cream

scant 1/2 cup unsalted pistachios, chopped

2 tbsp shredded fresh basil

To make the sauce, heat the oil in a large skillet. Add the scallions and garlic and cook for 1 minute, or until just softened.

Add the mushrooms and stir well, then cover and cook over low heat for 5 minutes, or until just softened but not browned.

Meanwhile, to cook the pasta, bring a large pan of lightly salted water to a boil. Add the tagliatelle, then bring back to a boil and cook for 3–5 minutes, or until tender but still firm to the bite. Drain thoroughly and return to the pan.

Going back to the sauce, add the spinach to the skillet and cook for 1–2 minutes. Add the cheese and heat until slightly melted. Stir in the cream and cook gently, without letting the mixture come to a boil, until warmed through.

Pour the sauce over the pasta. Season to taste with salt and pepper and mix well. Heat through gently, stirring constantly, for 2–3 minutes.

Transfer the pasta to a warmed serving dish and sprinkle with the pistachios and shredded basil. Garnish with the fresh basil sprigs and serve.

walnut & olive sauce

This vegetarian sauce is mouthwateringly light and excellent with pasta.
The quantities given here will make a lunch for four or an appetizer for six. *SERVES 4–6*

1 lb/450 g fresh fettucine

2 tbsp extra-virgin olive oil

2–3 tbsp chopped fresh parsley

sauce

2 thick slices whole-wheat bread,
crusts removed

1¹/₄ cups milk

2³/₄ cups shelled walnuts

2 garlic cloves, minced

²/₃ cup black olives, pitted

¹/₂ cup freshly grated Parmesan cheese

6 tbsp extra-virgin olive oil

salt and pepper

²/₃ cup heavy cream

To make the sauce, put the bread in a shallow dish. Pour over the milk and soak until the liquid has been absorbed.

Spread out the walnuts on a baking sheet and toast in a preheated oven, 375°F/190°C, for 5 minutes, or until golden. Let cool.

Put the soaked bread, shelled walnuts, minced garlic, black olives, grated Parmesan, and olive oil in a food processor and work to make a paste. Season to taste with salt and black pepper and then stir in the heavy cream.

To cook the pasta, bring a large pan of lightly salted water to a boil. Add the fettucine and half the oil and cook for 2–3 minutes, or until tender but still firm to the bite. Drain thoroughly and toss with the remaining olive oil.

Divide the cooked fettucine between individual serving plates and spoon the walnut and olive sauce on top. Sprinkle over the fresh parsley and serve.

cook's tip

Parmesan quickly loses its pungency and
bite when grated. It is better to buy small
quantities and grate it yourself. Wrapped in
foil, a piece will keep in the refrigerator for
several months.

basil & tomato sauce

Roasting the tomatoes gives a sweeter, smoother flavor to the sauce.
Italian plum or flavia tomatoes are ideal for this dish. *SERVES 4*

2 fresh rosemary sprigs

2 garlic cloves, unpeeled

1 lb/450 g tomatoes, halved and deseeded

1 tbsp olive oil

1 tbsp sun-dried tomato paste

12 fresh basil leaves, torn into pieces,
plus extra to garnish

salt and pepper

1lb 8 oz/675 g fresh farfalle or
12 oz/350 g dried

Place the rosemary, garlic, and tomatoes, skin-side up, in a shallow roasting pan and drizzle with the oil. Cook under a preheated broiler for about 20 minutes, or until the tomato skins have become slightly charred.

Peel the skin from the tomatoes. Coarsely chop the tomato flesh and place in a pan. Squeeze the pulp from the garlic cloves and mix with the tomato flesh and sun-dried tomato paste. Discard the rosemary. Stir the basil into the sauce. Season with salt and pepper to taste.

Cook the farfalle in a pan of lightly salted boiling water, according to the package directions, or until it is cooked through but still has bite. Drain the farfalle thoroughly.

Gently heat the tomato and basil sauce until warmed through.

Transfer the farfalle to serving plates and serve with the sauce, garnished with fresh basil leaves.

cook's tip

This sauce tastes just as good served
cold in a pasta salad.

variation

Try using a different shape of pasta, such as penne, for this recipe. Put it in an ovenproof dish, then top with some grated cheese and bake for a warming winter feast.

spicy tomato sauce

This deliciously fresh and slightly spicy tomato sauce is excellent
with pasta and makes a satisfying lunch or light supper. *SERVES 4*

To make the sauce, melt the butter in a pan. Add the onion and garlic and cook over low heat for 3–4 minutes.

Add the chilies and continue cooking for an additional 2 minutes.

Add the tomatoes and stock, then lower the heat and simmer, stirring occasionally, for 10 minutes.

Pour the sauce into a food processor and then blend for 1 minute, or until smooth. Alternatively, push the sauce through a strainer.

Return the sauce to the pan and add the tomato paste, sugar, and salt and pepper to taste. Gently reheat over low heat until piping hot.

To cook the pasta, put the tagliatelle in a pan of boiling water and cook according to the directions on the package, or until tender but still firm to the bite. Drain and transfer to serving plates. Serve immediately with the tomato sauce.

1 lb 8 oz/675 g fresh green and white
    tagliatelle, or 12 oz/350 g dried pasta

sauce

3 tbsp butter

1 onion, finely chopped

1 garlic clove, crushed

2 small red chilies, deseeded and diced

1 lb/450 g fresh tomatoes, skinned,
    deseeded and diced

generous 3/4 cup vegetable stock

2 tbsp tomato paste

1 tsp sugar

salt and pepper

mediterranean sauce

Delicious Mediterranean vegetables, cooked in rich tomato
sauce, make an ideal topping for nutty whole-wheat pasta. *SERVES 4*

12 oz/350 g dried whole-wheat spaghetti

1 tbsp olive oil

2 tbsp butter

sprigs of fresh basil, to garnish

olive bread, to serve

sauce

1 tbsp olive oil

1 large red onion, chopped

2 garlic cloves, finely chopped

1 tbsp lemon juice

4 baby eggplants, cut into fourths

2¹/₂ cups strained tomatoes

salt and pepper

2 tsp superfine sugar

2 tbsp tomato paste

**14 oz/400 g canned artichoke hearts,
drained and halved**

4 oz/115 g black olives, pitted

To make the sauce, heat the olive oil in a large skillet. Add the onion, garlic, lemon juice, and eggplants and then cook over low heat for 4–5 minutes, or until the onion and eggplants become lightly golden.

Pour in the strained tomatoes and season to taste with salt and black pepper, then stir in the superfine sugar and tomato paste. Bring to a boil, then lower the heat and simmer, stirring occasionally, for 20 minutes.

Gently stir in the artichoke hearts and black olives and cook for 5 minutes.

Meanwhile, cook the pasta. Bring a large pan of lightly salted water to a boil. Add the spaghetti and oil and cook for 7–8 minutes, or until tender but still firm to the bite.

Drain the spaghetti and toss with the butter. Transfer the spaghetti to a large serving dish.

Pour the vegetable sauce over the spaghetti and garnish with the sprigs of fresh basil. Serve immediately with olive bread.

fragrant eggplant sauce

Prepare the marinated eggplants well in advance so that, when you
are ready to eat, all you have to do is cook the pasta. *SERVES 4*

²/3 cup vegetable stock

²/3 cup white wine vinegar

2 tsp balsamic vinegar

3 tbsp olive oil

sprig of fresh oregano

1 lb/450 g eggplants, peeled and
thinly sliced

14 oz/400 g dried linguine

marinade

2 tbsp extra-virgin olive oil

2 garlic cloves, crushed

2 tbsp chopped fresh oregano

2 tbsp finely chopped roasted almonds

2 tbsp diced red bell pepper

2 tbsp lime juice

grated rind and juice of 1 orange

salt and pepper

Put the vegetable stock, wine vinegar, and balsamic vinegar into a pan and bring to a boil over low heat. Add 2 teaspoons of the olive oil and the sprig of fresh oregano and simmer gently for about 1 minute.

Add the eggplant slices to the pan, then remove from the heat and set aside for 10 minutes.

Meanwhile, to make the marinade, combine the oil, garlic, oregano, almonds, red bell pepper, lime juice, and orange rind and juice in a large bowl and season to taste with salt and pepper.

Using a slotted spoon, carefully remove the eggplant slices from the pan and drain well. Add the eggplant to the marinade, mixing well to coat. Cover with plastic wrap and set aside in the refrigerator for about 12 hours.

To cook the pasta, bring a large pan of lightly salted water to a boil. Add half of the remaining oil and the linguine. Bring back to a boil and cook for 8–10 minutes, or until just tender but still firm to the bite.

Drain the pasta thoroughly and toss with the remaining oil while it is still warm. Arrange the pasta on a serving plate with the eggplant slices and the marinade and serve immediately.

variation

Add 2 tablespoons of red wine vinegar to
the sauce and use as a dressing for a cold
pasta salad, if you wish.

chili & red bell pepper sauce

This roasted red bell pepper and chili sauce is sweet and spicy—the perfect combination for those who like to add a little spice to life! *SERVES 4*

1 lb 8 oz/675 g fresh pasta
or 12 oz/350 g dried pasta
fresh oregano leaves, to garnish

sauce

2 red bell peppers, halved and deseeded
1 small, fresh, red chili
4 tomatoes, halved
2 garlic cloves
¹/₃ cup ground almonds
scant ¹/₂ cup olive oil

To make the sauce, place the bell peppers, skin side up, on a baking sheet with the chili and tomatoes. Cook under a preheated broiler for 15 minutes, or until charred. After 10 minutes, turn the tomatoes over, skin side up. Put the bell peppers and chilies in a plastic bag and set aside for 10 minutes.

Peel the skins from the red bell peppers and chili and slice the flesh into strips. Peel the garlic, and peel and deseed the tomato halves.

Place the ground almonds on a baking sheet. Place under the broiler for 2–3 minutes until golden.

In a food processor, process the red bell peppers, chili, garlic, and tomatoes to make a purée. With the motor still running, slowly add the olive oil through the feeder tube to form a thick sauce. Alternatively, mash the mixture with a fork and beat in the olive oil, drop by drop.

Stir the toasted ground almonds into the mixture. Warm the sauce in a pan until it is heated.

To cook the pasta, bring a large pan of lightly salted water to a boil. Add the pasta, then bring back to a boil and cook for 3–5 minutes if using fresh pasta or 8–10 minutes if using dried pasta. Drain well and transfer to a serving dish. Pour over the sauce and toss to mix. Garnish with the fresh oregano leaves and serve.

green vegetable sauce

The different shapes and textures of the vegetables make a mouthwatering presentation in this light and summery dish. *SERVES 4*

8 oz/225 g dried gemelli or other dried pasta shapes

1 head broccoli, cut into florets

2 zucchini, sliced

8 oz/225 g asparagus spears

1 cup snow peas

1 cup frozen peas

¹/4 stick butter

3 tbsp vegetable stock

4 tbsp heavy cream

salt and pepper

freshly grated nutmeg

2 tbsp chopped fresh parsley

2 tbsp fresh Parmesan cheese shavings

Bring a large pan of lightly salted water to a boil over medium heat. Add the pasta and cook for 8–10 minutes, or until tender but still firm to the bite. Drain thoroughly and return to the pan, then cover and keep warm.

Steam the broccoli, zucchini, asparagus spears, and snow peas over a pan of boiling salted water until they are just starting to soften. Remove from the heat and refresh in cold water. Drain and reserve.

Bring a small pan of lightly salted water to a boil over medium heat. Add the frozen peas and cook for 3 minutes. Drain the peas and refresh in cold water, then drain again. Reserve with the other vegetables.

Heat the butter and vegetable stock in a pan over medium heat. Add all of the vegetables, reserving a few of the asparagus spears, and toss carefully with a wooden spoon until they have heated through, taking care not to break them up.

Stir in the cream and heat through without bringing to a boil. Season to taste with salt, pepper, and nutmeg.

Transfer the pasta to a warmed serving dish and stir in the chopped parsley. Spoon over the vegetable sauce and sprinkle over the Parmesan cheese. Arrange the reserved asparagus spears in a pattern on the top and serve.

cook's tip

You can use lime juice instead of the
lemon juice. Since limes are usually
smaller, squeeze the juice from 2 fruits.

hot zucchini sauce

This is a really fresh-tasting sauce, made with zucchini and cream.
This dish is ideal with a crisp white wine and some crusty bread. *SERVES 4*

To make the sauce, use a swivel-bladed vegetable peeler to slice the zucchini into thin ribbons.

Heat the oil in a skillet and cook the garlic for 30 seconds.

Add the zucchini and cook over low heat, stirring, for 5–7 minutes.

Stir in the basil, chilies, lemon juice, cream, and Parmesan and season to taste. Keep warm over a very low heat.

To cook the pasta, bring a large pan of lightly salted water to a boil. Add the pasta, then bring back to a boil and cook for 8–10 minutes, or until tender but still firm to the bite. Drain thoroughly and put the pasta in a warm serving bowl.

Pile the zucchini sauce on top of the pasta and serve with crusty bread.

8 oz/225 g dried tagliatelle

crusty bread, to serve

sauce

1 lb 8 oz/675 g zucchini

6 tbsp olive oil

3 garlic cloves, crushed

3 tbsp chopped fresh basil

2 fresh red chilies, deseeded and sliced

juice of 1 large lemon

5 tbsp light cream

4 tbsp grated Parmesan cheese

salt and pepper

index